SOUTH AFRICA

...BOOK

...richs

...ress®
...r Publishing
...g Kong Sydney
...ecticut

Reading Consultant
Linda Cornwell
Learning Resource Consultant
Indiana Department of
Education

An outdoor market

Library of Congress Cataloging-in-Publication Data

Heinrichs, Ann.
    South Africa / by Ann Heinrichs.
    p.   cm. — (A true book)
    Includes bibliographical references and index.
    Summary: A basic overview of the history, geography, climate, and culture of South Africa.
    ISBN 0-516-20340-1 (lib. bdg.)   0-516-26176-2 (pbk.)
    1. South Africa—Juvenile literature. [1. South Africa.] I. Title. II. Series.
DT1719.H45   1997
968—dc20   96-31634
                                                                          CIP
                                                                          AC

Contents

Deserts, Mountains, and Veld

South Africa is one of the largest countries in Africa. It covers about 471,000 square miles (1,221,000 square kilometers). South Africa lies at the southern tip of Africa. Along its west coast is the Atlantic Ocean. The country's east coast faces the Indian Ocean.

South Africa borders the countries of Namibia, Botswana, Zimbabwe, Mozambique, and Swaziland. It also completely surrounds the country of Lesotho. A finger of land on the southern coast of South Africa is called the Cape of Good Hope.

South Africa has a beautiful and varied landscape. The central region is a large

The central region of South Africa is called the veld.

plateau called the veld, meaning grassy plain. It is high and flat, with lush grasslands. Along the plateau's edge are mountains called the Great Escarpment.

The Kalahari Desert in the north continues into Botswana

and Namibia. The Namib Desert lies along the Atlantic coast. Sandy beaches and rocky shores line the south and east coasts of South Africa.

Many national parks and game reserves protect South Africa's wild animals. Visitors may see lions, zebras, giraffes, elephants, and rhinoceroses.

South Africa is in the Southern Hemisphere, south of the equator. Its seasons are the opposite of those in North

Many beautiful beaches (left) are found in South Africa. Visitors to national parks in South Africa can get up-close views of the wild animals (right).

America. For example, January is in the warm season and July is in the cool season. Temperatures in South Africa are moderate, without extreme heat or cold.

People of Many Cultures

About three of every four people in South Africa are Africans, usually called blacks. The largest ethnic groups are the Zulu and Xhosa. The Sotho and Tswana people are the next largest groups.

About one of every seven South Africans is white. More than half the white people

People from many different ethnic groups live in South Africa.

are Afrikaners. Their ancestors were settlers from The Netherlands, France and Germany. Their language, called Afrikaans, is a form of Dutch. Other whites—descended from British, Irish, or Scottish people—speak English.

More than half the white people in South Africa are Afrikaners.

South Africa's Asian people are descendants of workers brought from India and Malaysia in the late 1800s. Most live in the eastern province of KwaZulu-Natal.

South Africans of mixed heritage are called Coloreds.

Their ancestors are a mixture of blacks, Asians, and whites. Most of South Africa's Coloreds speak Afrikaans. They live mainly in Northern and Western Cape provinces.

People of mixed heritage are called Coloreds.

Cape Town is one of three capital cities in South Africa.

Cape Town, on the southern coast, is South Africa's largest city. Durban, on the east coast, is the second largest. Other major cities are Johannesburg, Soweto, and Pretoria. South Africa has three capitals: Cape Town, Pretoria, and Bloemfontein.

The Zulu

About seven million Zulu live in South Africa. They speak a Bantu language. About half of the Zulu people are farmers and cattle herders. They live in round mud huts with thatched roofs. Other Zulu live in urban areas and work in the cities or mines.

The Early Days

The people of South Africa come from many different backgrounds. Africans, or blacks, have lived there for more than two thousand years.

Descendants of South Africa's white settlers have a history of more than three hundred years. Millions of

Many varied and diverse groups of people can all be called South Africans.

South Africans belong to Asian and mixed ethnic groups.

Around the year A.D. 300, Bantu-speaking people from central Africa began moving into the region that is now known as South Africa. In 1488,

Portuguese explorers arrived in South Africa in 1488.

explorers sailed from Portugal to the Cape of Good Hope. They were the first Europeans to arrive in South Africa.

In 1652, traders of the Dutch East India Company set up a fort on the Cape. This became known as Cape Town. Later,

French people seeking religious freedom came to South Africa. People from Germany arrived, too. Together, these settlers were called Boers—a Dutch word meaning farmers. Later they were named Afrikaners.

In 1652, ships brought Dutch traders who set up a fort on the Cape of Good Hope.

Each year, Afrikaners re-create the Great Trek taken by the Boers to protest British rule.

In 1814, Great Britain took control of South Africa and established two colonies— Cape Colony and Natal. The Boers, who disliked British rule, moved farther north in 1836. This journey is known as the Great Trek.

Building a New South Africa

For most of the nation's history, South Africa was ruled by a white minority. Blacks, who greatly outnumbered the whites, were denied many rights. Only white people were allowed to vote. Non-white groups lived

Cape Town's City Hall

under South Africa's policy of apartheid, which means separateness.

South Africa's blacks wanted to be able to vote and to have representatives in the country's government. In 1912, several black leaders banded together to work for equal rights. This group became known as the African National Congress (ANC) party. In 1960, the ANC was banned in South Africa.

The African National Congress was formed by black leaders who worked to end apartheid.

In 1962, Nelson Mandela, a leader of the ANC, was sentenced to life in prison.

Meanwhile, many apartheid laws had been passed. These laws controlled where non-whites could live, work, and travel. Blacks were required to live in poor regions called black homelands.

Many countries throughout the world began to cut off trade with South Africa to protest apartheid. Many foreign

Black homelands (top) were areas where the apartheid government ordered blacks to live. Black South Africans' protests against apartheid (bottom) were supported by other countries.

companies closed and left the country. These moves hurt South Africa's economy. Its leaders got rid of some apartheid laws in the 1980s, but many more changes were needed.

In 1990, President F. W. de Klerk began major reforms. Blacks were no longer confined to the homelands. The ANC was free to operate, and Nelson Mandela was released from prison. By then, Mandela had become a hero to anti-apartheid South Africans.

President F. W. de Klerk (left) and Nelson Mandela (center) took part in a South African peace conference in 1996.

Mandela and de Klerk began meetings to talk about how to improve life in South Africa.

In 1993, South Africans adopted a new constitution. It granted equal rights to all citizens of all races. Mandela and de Klerk were awarded the

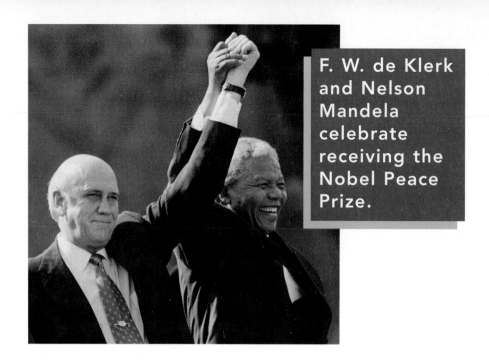

F. W. de Klerk and Nelson Mandela celebrate receiving the Nobel Peace Prize.

Nobel Peace Prize for their work. In 1994, for the first time, South Africans of all races were allowed to vote. They elected Nelson Mandela as president. He immediately began working to build a better South Africa.

Nelson Mandela

Nelson Mandela was born in South Africa in 1918. He joined the ANC in 1944. Mandela became a well-known leader of protests against apartheid. He was imprisoned in 1962, and sentenced to death in 1964. He became a symbol of black South Africans' struggle for equality. In 1990, Mandela was finally released from prison. He became the first black president of South Africa in 1994.

How People Live

About half of South Africa's blacks live in cities. Many live in black townships where the housing and living conditions are poor. Before 1991, children of different races had to attend separate schools. Now public schools are integrated. This means that

An integrated classroom in Cape Town

students of all races may go to any public school.

Since apartheid ended, blacks have begun to move into neighborhoods that used to be all white. Some blacks continue to live in the former homelands and to follow their

Zulu and other ethnic groups honor their heritage by wearing traditional clothing.

ethnic traditions. Various groups wear traditional clothing of bright woven cloth.

Asians of Indian ancestry also follow many traditional customs. Women wear the sari, the flowing dress of Indian women.

Most white South Africans live in cities or suburbs. Their standard of living is similar to that of upper-middle-class people in Europe and the United States. Some live in beautiful homes with lush gardens, high walls, and flowering trees.

Many beautiful homes can be found throughout South Africa.

Visitors to South Africa enjoy a wide variety of ethnic foods.

South African food is quite varied. Malaysians make *bobotie*, a spicy ground-meat dish. Indians enjoy curry—eggs, meat, fish, or vegetables in a spicy sauce. Afrikaners like *boerewors* (sausages), and strips of chewy, dried meat called

biltong are a favorite snack.
Among blacks, a basic food is a
corn stew called mealies.

The British brought the
sports of cricket, rugby, tennis,
and golf to South Africa. Soccer,
called association football, is a
very popular sport.

Many South Africans'
favorite sport is soccer.

Economy and Jobs

South Africa's economy is the strongest in Africa. But most of South Africa's non-whites work at low-paying jobs. Whites hold most of the high-paying jobs and own most of the large businesses. Almost one-half of all South Africans are unemployed, and most of these are blacks. But there

South Africa has a strong economy because of its many successful businesses and industries.

are also many wealthy profes-
sional people among South
Africa's non-whites.

South Africa's factories and
farms produce almost every-
thing the country needs.
Factory goods are South

Many South Africans work hard in factories (top) or on farms (bottom right). Mining (bottom left) is difficult work, but South African mines contain huge amounts of gold, diamonds, and coal.

Africa's most important products. They include chemicals, clothing, machines, steel, and cars. Farms in South Africa raise apples, citrus fruit, corn, potatoes, wheat, sugarcane, and many other products. Sheep and cattle graze on the lush grasslands, and sheep's wool is an important export.

Mining is also a major part of the economy. South Africa is the world's leading producer of gold, chromium, and vanadium. Diamonds and uranium are also important products. More than half of Africa's coal is in South Africa.

Culture and Arts

Many traditional African arts and crafts still exist in South Africa. They include handwoven blankets and wall hangings, wood carvings, pottery, and jewelry. Some ethnic groups decorate the walls and door-ways of their homes with colorful murals (wall paintings).

Cape Dutch architecture (left) was developed in South Africa. Colorful murals (right) decorate many South African homes.

In the cities, many public buildings look like buildings that can be found in Europe. South Africans also developed an architectural style of their own, called Cape Dutch.

Music is an important part of South African culture. The Afrikaners' *Boeremusiek* is a popular style of folk song. In tribal regions, blacks play traditional music on drums, reeds, horns, and xylophones. Their songs and dances relate to tribal life and customs. Blacks in the cities enjoy *lo jazz*, a mixture of African and Western music.

South Africa has experienced many changes during

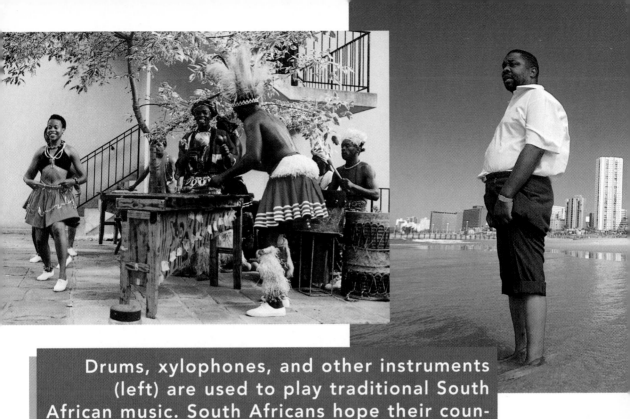

Drums, xylophones, and other instruments (left) are used to play traditional South African music. South Africans hope their country will continue to grow and prosper (right).

its history. The country continues to change, and South Africa's leaders are working hard to make a better life for all South Africans.

To Find Out More

Here are some additional resources to help you learn more about the nation of South Africa:

 **Books**

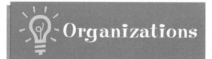 **Organizations**

Canesso, Claudia. **Places and Peoples of the World: South Africa.** Chelsea House, 1988.

Brandenburg, Jim. **Sand & Fog: Adventures in Southern Africa.** Walker & Co., 1994.

Isadora, Rachel. **At The Crossroads.** Morrow, 1994.

Dell, Pamela. **Nelson Mandela: Freedom for South Africa.** Children's Press, 1994.

Johannesburg Chamber of Commerce
JCC House
27 Owl Street, 6th Floor
Auckland Park, 2006
Republic of South Africa

South Africa Consulate-General
50 N. La Cienega Boulevard
Suite 300
Beverly Hills, CA 90211
e-mail: safrcgla@link2 southafrica.com

Online Sites

About South Africa

http://www.geocities.com/ SiliconValley/2193/saf1.html

General information and statistics about South Africa, as well as links to other related sites

Ananzi's Catalogue: Sports

http://www.ananzi.co.za/ catalogue/sports.html

Learn about cricket, cycling, fishing, rugby, horse racing, soccer, underwater hockey, and many other sports that South Africans enjoy.

Boer Nation's Page

http://www.boer.co.za/boer

You'll find plenty of information about the Boers and their homelands in South Africa, including history, geography, and pictures. Visit Pretoria, Natal, Orange Free State, Transvaal, and more.

South Africa

http://osprey.unisa.ac.za/ south-africa/images/ south-africa/home.html

This site features beautiful pictures, as well as links to hundreds of other sites about South Africa.

Important Words

ancestors relatives who lived long ago

descendants present-day relatives of people who lived long ago

economy a country's wealth, based on the goods and services it produces

export a product that is sold to another country

ethnic relating to a person's race

heritage the culture and history of a people's past

reforms changes or improvements

suburbs communities that lie outside of a city

traditions customs that people have followed for a long time

Index

Meet the Author

Ann Heinrichs grew up in Arkansas and lives in Chicago, Illinois. She has written more than twenty books about American, Asian, and African history and culture. She has also written numerous newspaper, magazine, and encyclopedia articles.

Besides the United States, she has traveled in Europe, North Africa, the Middle East, and east Asia. The desert is her favorite terrain.

Ms. Heinrichs holds bachelor's and master's degrees in piano performance. For relaxation, she practices chi gung and t'ai chi.